BISON

Jack Ballard

D1607423

FALCONGUIDES

GUILFORD, CONNECTICUT
HELENA, MONTANA

AN IMPRINT OF GLOBE PEQUOT PRESS

To buy books in quantity for corporate use
or incentives, call **(800) 962-0973**
or e-mail **premiums@GlobePequot.com**.

FALCONGUIDES®

FalconGuides is an imprint of Globe Pequot Press.
Falcon, FalconGuides, and Outfit Your Mind are registered trademarks of Morris Book Publishing, LLC.

Interior photos by Jack Ballard unless noted otherwise.

Project Editor: David Legere
Text Design: Sheryl P. Kober
Layout Artist: Sue Murray

Library of Congress Cataloging-in-Publication Data is available on file.

ISBN 978-0-7627-8101-0

Printed in the United States of America

10 9 8 7 6 5 4 3 2 1

To my former teachers at the Three Forks Schools who gave me the ability to read, write, and think, most especially those who advanced my appreciation for, and knowledge of, the natural world.

Contents

Contents

Chapter 6: Bison and Humans

Acknowledgments

Had it not been for a handful of people who captured and preserved bison in the late 19th century, the species may have become extinct in the contiguous United States. All who admire the bison are indebted to these individuals. Those who played a direct role in capturing bison are: Samuel "Walking Coyote" Wells, a native hunter of the Pend d'Orielle tribe (Montana); James McKay and Charles Alloway (Canada); Charles Goodnight (Texas); Frederick Dupree (South Dakota); and Charles "Buffalo" Jones (Kansas).

Special thanks to Brendan Moynahan, Ph.D, lead biologist at the National Bison Range for reviewing and making helpful comments on the manuscript.

Introduction

On a warm July afternoon, I sat on a hard wooden bench with a host of other tourists, waiting for the eruption of Old Faithful Geyser, one of Yellowstone National Park's premier attractions. The bench was one of many arrayed in semicircular rows, affording a front row seat to one of nature's unique spectacles.

As the estimated time for the eruption neared, the benches filled to capacity. But there was a distraction. A bull bison grazing between the arena and the geyser slowly lumbered toward the audience, its head down, teeth grinding, apparently oblivious of the seated humans. The bull came closer to the benches. People yielded their seats in deference to the hulking animal, though it seemed to sense only the earth between its hooves, the stems of grass between its teeth. All the humans yielded to the bison, save one.

One chubby, middle-aged man with a sunburned countenance, safari-type shorts, and a camera slung over his shoulder wasn't about to be buffaloed. He kept his front row seat as the bison edged closer, though the ring of empty seats around him steadily grew. Smugness radiated from his erect posture, no doubt emanating from his superior courage in the face of all those other cowardly tourists.

Some 50 feet from Mr. Smug, the bison charged without warning. In the blink of an eye, as hundreds of people gasped in alarm, the immense creature went from a mindless, grazing hulk to a wild-eyed, snorting behemoth. Faster than I could contemplate the consequences, its massive head and curved, dirt-stained horns confronted the previously defiant human at a distance measured in inches.

The animal's intention was clearly to intimidate its challenger, not injure him. It succeeded masterfully. Limbs flailing, the terrified gentleman fell backward from his seat, scrabbling about in the dirt like a frenzied centipede. He proceeded to crawl frantically under the benches away from the bison, standing only when he reached the host of people with sense enough to give the bull its space. The mood of the crowd instantly changed from consternation to mirth. When the geyser erupted minutes later, the previously truculent fellow was noticeably absent from the crowd.

A humorous instance, that experience forever changed my attitude toward bison. The knowledge that they are unpredictable, powerful, and supremely athletic beasts when provoked was emphasized in spades. But a curiosity about their natural history and behavior awakened as well. In the three decades since that idle summer afternoon, I've had the opportunity to observe bison in dozens of habitats in numerous locations, most often in state and national parks. Their life seems one of boring routine, occasionally punctuated with notable events and memorable behaviors. It is in those moments that they are among the most fascinating creatures in North America. I offer this book with the hope that the reader's respect and appreciation for these iconic creatures of the Old West will grow with the turning of each page.

CHAPTER 1

Names and Faces

Names and Visual Description

Bison or *American bison* is the formal name of the largest terrestrial (land-dwelling) animal in North America. In the common language these animals are more often called *buffalo*.

Which name, *bison* or *buffalo*, is correct? Although some individuals make a fuss over referring to these animals as *bison*, either term is acceptable. In scientific circles and formal biological contexts, *bison* is the preferred term. However, most experts agree that in common conversation either *bison* or *buffalo* is an appropriate name for these imposing animals.

Male bison are called *bulls*. Bull bison are the largest land animal in North America.

With an average height at the humped shoulder that interestingly equals about the average height of an adult human in the United States, bison are tall, but bulky-appearing animals. Bison are brown, but their coloration is not completely uniform. Their head, neck, and lower legs are usually quite dark, frequently the color of strong black coffee. Their shoulders and hump are sometimes tan or even golden in appearance. Their ribs and hindquarters are medium brown. However, coloration on an adult bison's body may vary from animal to animal and can change from season to season. Some adult bison exhibit a consistent medium brown color that doesn't change much over their entire body. Other animals have tan hair that extends from the base of their neck all the way to their rump. I've seen bison with very dark brown legs and heads that display golden brown hair on the rest of their massive frames.

Male bison are known as *bulls,* females are called *cows.* Viewed from the side, bison have a noticeable hump that extends above their shoulders. Seen from the front, their head appears broad and massive. Both bulls and cows have horns that sprout from the sides of their skull near the top and curve upward. The horns of cows tend to curve up and in, while the horns of bulls curve up and out. Their tail extends from their rump about halfway to the ground or around the level of their hocks (the prominent joint at the midpoint of hoofed animals' rear legs). The hair at the end of their tail is often thicker or tufted. Bison have a prominent "beard" of hair that hangs below their chin. They also sport long hair below their neck and on the rear of the upper portion of their front legs. The hair on their head, neck, and shoulders is longer and curly in comparison to the hair found on the rest of their body. This is especially noticeable on large bulls during the summer months.

Related Species in North America

To the trained eye, there is no other wild animal in North America easily mistaken for a bison. The animals' sheer size, characteristic shape, and prominent hump give them a profile that is much different than the other herbivores with which they share their range. However, novice wildlife watchers, like early settlers to the eastern United States, might confuse bison with two of the continent's other large hoofed animals.

The ranges of moose and bison overlap in some places in the Rocky Mountains, Canada, and Alaska. Moose are similar in height to bison and somewhat the same color, although moose usually appear more uniformly dark brown or black across their bodies when compared to bison. Bison lack the prominent, round ears that thrust from the top of the moose's head. Moose look lanky, with legs that are long in comparison to the bulk of their body. By contrast, bison appear to have shorter legs that seem stubby in relation to their behemoth bodies. Although moose have an evident hump on their shoulders similar to bison, the top of a moose's rump is just slightly shorter than its shoulders. By contrast, the hump over a bison's shoulders sits much higher than its rump. The bison's massive head is carried lower than its shoulders when standing; the top of a moose's head is higher than the apex of its shoulders. Male moose (bulls) carry flattish, branched antlers for much of the year; female moose (cows) have neither horns nor antlers. The shorter horns of the bison, which taper to a pointed tip, look very different from the antlers of even a small bull moose, which usually broaden as they extend from the animal's skull. A moose's tail is stubby and hardly noticeable, unlike the longer tail of a bison.

Elk, another hoofed mammal of notable size, share ranges with bison in many places, such as Yellowstone and Grand Teton National Parks in Wyoming, Theodore Roosevelt National Park in North Dakota, and Custer State Park in South Dakota, to name a few. Elk are significantly shorter than bison. Like bison, the elk's body is covered in hair in shades of brown. However, elk have a large, prominent patch of fur on their rump that is quite yellow. Elk have a very short tail, more like a moose than a bison. Young male elk (bulls) have antlers that are over a foot long; mature bull elk have antlers that sport multiple tines and are commonly 3 to 4 feet in length. Female elk (cows) lack the horns seen on both cow and bull bison.

Moose and elk might be mistaken for bison at a distance. The towering hump and noticeably lower hindquarters of the bison contrast with the straighter backline of elk and moose.

Musk oxen—a large, hairy animal of the far north—could potentially be mistaken for bison. Musk oxen are creatures of the Arctic tundra. Their range is more than 500 miles to the north of the nearest bison found in Alaska or Canada. The musk oxen's horns are larger than a bison's and curve downward instead of up. Musk oxen have exceptionally long hair that extends nearly to the ground, obscuring most of their front and hind legs.

Of the animals in North America, bison are most closely related to domestic cattle. American bison share the *bison* genus with one other species of European bison. However, they are also very closely related to members of the *bos* genus, which includes domestic cattle, gaur, yak, kouprey, and banteng. Banteng, gaur, and kouprey are wild cattle-like creatures that are native to southern and southeastern Asia. Yak are a long-haired cattle-like species of south central and eastern Asia. Because bison can mate and produce fertile offspring with every species of the *bos* genus,

Buffalo are more closely related to domestic cattle than any other animal in North America.

many biologists feel that bison and these other cattle-like species should be included in a single genus. Ranchers who captured and maintained bison with their cattle herds sometimes deliberately interbred bison and cattle to the extent that most "wild" bison found in the United States at the present time carry some (generally very small) genetic influence from domestic cattle.

Subspecies

American bison are near relatives of the wisent or European bison. The scientific or Latin name for American bison is *Bison bison*. European bison bear the formal name *Bison bonasus*. Like their North American counterparts, wisent are the largest land-dwelling wild animal in Europe. The bison of North America and Europe are generally similar in appearance. However, European bison are a bit taller on average. They also have slightly longer horns and tails. The hair on the frontal portions of the North American bison's head, neck, and shoulders tends to be longer than that on the wisent. Additionally, wisent carry their heads higher—a feature that better enables them in browsing on shrubs and woody plants—than the low-slung head of the American bison, which feeds almost exclusively on grass and sedges.

In addition to their biological similarities, American and European bison share a common history with humans. Both species were hunted to near extinction, with surviving populations originating from remnant herds that numbered a tiny fraction of their historic numbers. Wisent have been reintroduced into the wild in select areas of several countries in Europe, a pattern similar to the reintroduction of bison at various national, state, and provincial parks and wildlife refuges in the United States and Canada.

Within North America some biologists recognize two sub-species of bison: plains bison (*Bison bison bison*) and wood bison (*Bison bison athabascae*). Others believe that wood bison and plains bison should not be recognized as separate subspecies. Wood bison are found in Alaska and Canada. Plains bison are found primarily in the contiguous United States.

Some biologists believe wood bison, like this one in northern British Columbia, should be classified as a separate subspecies. Others believe wood bison and plains bison are the same.

Historically, wood bison roamed throughout much of the boreal forest regions of Alaska and western Canada. Genetically pure wood bison were considered by many to be extinct by the early twentieth century, due to interbreeding with plains bison. In 1957, however, a herd of around 200 animals was discovered in Alberta, Canada, that was thought to be an isolated, genetically pure strain of wood bison. The Canadian government developed and implemented a program to preserve and propagate these bison. Today free-ranging wood bison are found in a limited number of areas in Alaska and Canada.

The largest specimens of North American bison belong to the wood bison subspecies. Wood bison bulls are usually about 10 percent heavier than plains bison bulls. Large wood bison bulls can weigh over 2,200 pounds and stand over 6 feet tall at the shoulders, making them the largest land animal in North America. When viewed from the side, the prominent hump on a wood bison sits in front of its shoulders. Wood bison have thick, woolly hair on their head and shoulders. They are commonly believed to have thicker hair, longer legs, and a more pointed beard than plains bison.

Plains bison are the subspecies that originally inhabited the vast grasslands of North America. The current existence of plains bison can be traced to a remnant herd in Yellowstone National Park and a few private herds that were kept from extinction in the late 1800s. The plains bison's hump sits slightly behind its front shoulders when viewed from the side. Plains bison are often described as being somewhat shorter than wood bison with a slightly blockier appearance.

Physical Characteristics

Reported averages vary somewhat depending on the source, but most bison bulls mature at around 1,800 to 2,000 pounds. Bison are a species that displays significant sexual dimorphism. *Sexual dimorphism* is a fancy biological term that simply refers to the fact that one gender within the species (usually males, but sometimes females) is significantly larger than the other. In the

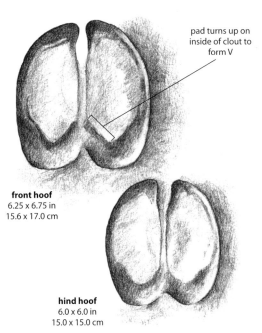

pad turns up on inside of clout to form V

front hoof
6.25 x 6.75 in
15.6 x 17.0 cm

hind hoof
6.0 x 6.0 in
15.0 x 15.0 cm

female horn

male horn

CATTLE POLLUTION.
SHOULD WE CARE?

Virtually all bison in the United States can be traced back to two sources of animals in the late nineteenth century. A tiny herd of some thirty bison persisted in the mountains of northwestern Wyoming after receiving protection from hunting through the creation of Yellowstone National Park. Elsewhere, as bison were nearing extinction on the plains, a handful of ranchers captured wild bison and began breeding them in captivity. Historical records indicate five such captive herds were established with a total of around eighty animals.

While these ranchers loved their bison, they also saw them as a means of improving their domestic cattle herds. Bison and cattle can interbreed, although with difficulty. Mating between the two species does not normally occur under natural conditions and often requires considerable effort by ranchers seeking to produce bison-cattle offspring. A bison-cattle crossbred animal, the ranchers speculated, would be much more hardy and better able to survive the harsh winters that sometimes decimated cattle herds on the prairies. Thus, some of the cattlemen tinkered with various crossbreeding schemes between their bison and cattle.

Ultimately, the experiments went nowhere from a commercial or agricultural standpoint. However, they did introduce cattle genes into these bison herds in varying degrees. Animals from these five sources were used to populate various state and national parks, along with other governmental reserves where bison began to flourish. Bison that can ultimately be traced to these five sources were also brought to Yellowstone to supplement its herd.

Advances in genetic testing over the past few decades reveal that most free-ranging and captive bison display genetic markers of domestic cattle. The extent of this genetic "introgression" varies from place to place. In no case is it significant enough to change the appearance of the bison. In fact, a crossbred bison-cattle animal bred back to a bison will lose readily identifiable features of a cow in just a generation or two. However, scientists wonder if the tiny, but persistent genetic influence of cattle makes a difference in existing bison.

Perhaps it does. One study compared bison from two herds, one in a nutritionally rich environment and another in a nutritionally stressed environment. Researchers found that bison displaying traces of cattle genes in their mitochondrial DNA did not weigh as much and had a smaller frame than bison whose DNA did not contain cattle genetics.

To the human eye, the trace cattle genes intermingled in bison herds in our state and national parks is undetectable. Typical viewers of bison in the likes of Yellowstone, Wind Cave, Badlands, Grand Teton, or Theodore Roosevelt National Parks have no inkling of the cattle genes present in the large animals in front of them. Maybe it doesn't matter. But if new herds are established on additional public reserves in our nation, the issue may cause debate between some biologists who would like to see only "pure" bison introduced in new public areas and those who feel the greater genetic diversity offered by animals that exhibit slight introgression of cattle genes is ultimately better for the species.

Bull bison (on right) are nearly twice as heavy as cows (on left).

case of bison, the variance in weight between bulls and cows is extreme. Bulls are about 75 to 100 percent heavier than cows. The average cow matures at around 900 to 1,100 pounds. Most adult bull bison stand approximately 6 feet at the shoulders. Cows are about a foot shorter.

Baby bison are called *calves*. A bison calf begins life a much different color than its parents. Bison calves are reddish in color, with lighter, nearly cream-colored hair on their bellies and the inside of their legs. The unusual-colored coat of the young bison is shed at around 2 months of age. After shedding, youngsters mostly appear as smaller versions of adults, with much tinier horns.

Chapter 2

Range and Habitat

Historic Range

Bison once ranged over much of North America, from northern Mexico to Alaska. Prior to the middle of the second millennium (around 1500), most of the contiguous United States held bison herds. Bison were absent from heavily forested areas along the Pacific coast and the desert regions of the Southwest. They did not inhabit Maine and were found only in the southern portion of the

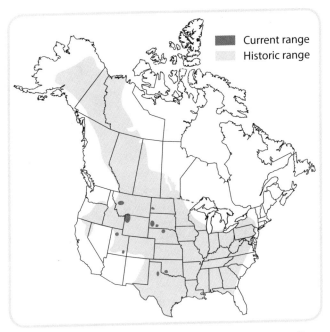

Current range
Historic range

Location of major bison herds in the contiguous United States in relation to historic bison range in North America.

other New England states, probably in small numbers. There was something of a bison buffer along the Atlantic coast. The range of bison was normally found at least 50 to 100 miles from the coastline. Bison were found in the Southeast, perhaps as far south as northern Florida, but some debate has existed regarding the historic range of bison in this area for over a century. As early as the late 1800s, experts argued whether bison actually inhabited southern portions of Louisiana or Georgia. They also squabbled over the historic status of bison in Florida and Alabama.

Estimating the historic range of bison illustrates an interesting aspect of history. Eyewitness accounts of various animals by early explorers are a common way to establish that a certain species lived in a particular area. However, in the case of Europeans

Bison once roamed over much of what is now the United States, but they were most numerous on the prairies.

exploring North America in first few centuries following the "discovery" of the New World by Christopher Columbus in 1492, they didn't always know what they were viewing. Many North American wildlife species are absent from Europe. The names given to North American animals in the journals of early observers weren't always consistent, nor were there differentiations among species. For example, suppose an intrepid traveler saw an animal that he described as large, dark, hairy, and cloven-hoofed. The creature could be a bison, but it could also be a moose.

Historical records of nonnative adventurers encountering bison in North America during the fifteenth and sixteenth centuries are few, but they do help to establish the nearly coast-to-coast historic range of these large, imposing animals. Alvar Nuñez Cabeza de Vaca, a Spanish explorer, was shipwrecked in the Gulf of Mexico around 1530. He journeyed inland through what is now Texas, observing large herds of bison at least three times. He ate bison, commenting favorably on the taste of the meat. Members of Coronado's Spanish expedition viewed bison on the southern plains about a decade later, somewhere in the region of the Texas panhandle.

Perhaps the first encounter with bison by nonnative peoples on the East Coast occurred in 1612. On March 18, Captain Samuel Argoll, an Englishman, anchored his ship off the coast of Virginia. He then presumably traveled up the Potomac River. Somewhere not too far from the present-day location of Washington, D.C., he happened upon a herd of bison. His Indian guides killed two of the animals for meat. In a letter to a friend back in England, Argoll commented on the pleasant taste of the meat and the fact that the buffalo weren't as wild as other animals he had encountered in the American wilderness.

In December 1679, Father Louis Hennepin saw bison on the Illinois River in the vicinity of what is now Peoria. The French priest had journeyed along the Saint Lawrence River and across the Great Lakes region on an exploratory trip of the area. He killed an old bull buffalo and noted the difficulty his party had in retrieving the animal from the mud.

As scouts traveled westward from the settlements along the Atlantic coast in the 1700s, they increasingly came into contact with bison. Buffalo were discovered in North Carolina and Virginia, and as Europeans began exploring the Appalachian Mountains, they found bison from southern New York to Georgia. After the Revolutionary War westward settlement accelerated. Pioneers discovered bison with each westward expansion, gladly killing them for food or their hides. As they went, the settlers quickly exterminated the bison.

The story of the decline of American bison from their historic range has often been oversimplified. A common estimate of the number of bison in North America prior to European settlement is sixty million animals. However, recent scientific estimates of the carrying capacity of bison range based on such variables as rainfall, grassland types, competition with other grazers, and historic US Department of Agriculture (USDA) livestock census data indicate a maximum figure of around thirty million. One scholarly source merely reports that bison in the tens of millions historically roamed North America.

Unbridled hunting by market hunters and extermination campaigns intended to eliminate the major food supply for Native American peoples during the mid- to late 1800s are the most frequently cited reasons for the near extinction of the bison. But the equation isn't quite so simple. Prior to widespread killing by Europeans, native hunters had already exerted some pressure on bison populations. When American Indians acquired horses in the 1600s, cultures soon developed that depended heavily upon bison for food, shelter, and other necessities of life. The horse gave the native peoples increased efficiency in killing bison. Historians note that by 1800, Comanche Indians were starving for a lack of bison on the southern plains and that soon thereafter bison disappeared from the region west of the Rocky Mountains. Biologists variously cite pressure from native hunters, exotic bovine diseases, competition with wild horses, predation, drought, and other natural phenomena as instrumental in the decline of the bison. However, most agree that the widespread elimination of herds by market hunters supported by railway development in the latter decades of the 1800s was the most significant cause of the near-extinction of the bison.

By 1835 bison had disappeared east of the Mississippi River. Two buffalo were killed by Sioux Indians in northern Wisconsin in 1832, perhaps the final chapter in the animals' history east of this great riverine dividing line in America. However, bison were still wildly abundant on the Great Plains and westward to the Rocky Mountains. Competent observers in the 1860s in Kansas claimed to have been within viewing distance of 100,000 or more bison from a single hilltop.

By 1880 the innumerable herds of bison on the plains had nearly vanished. Unbridled hunting of bison for their hide, meat, and bones, along with aggressive efforts to suppress bison numbers as a means to subdue American Indian tribes, wiped out buffalo by the hundreds of thousands per year. Naturalist William Hornaday estimated in 1913 that no more than 1,300 bison existed in the wild or captivity by 1889 in the United States and Canada. In 1975 a respected biologist theorized that only 85 bison remained in the wild in the United States in 1888. Shortly thereafter, the only free-ranging vestige of the tens of millions of bison once found in the United States was a tiny herd of some 30 animals eking out a precarious existence in the mountain valleys of Yellowstone National Park.

Current Range

Describing the current range of bison in North America is difficult. It's not that bison are hard to locate or live in terrain inhospitable to human observers. Rather, one's assessment of the buffalo's current range depends on how the author handles the numerous bison that are private property, classified as livestock, and range exclusively on private lands. Bison "ranches" are found all over the country. In some states small herds are owned by universities or conservation organizations. In other places bison are raised and slaughtered for their meat as an agricultural product. Around 30,000 bison are kept as wildlife or for conservation purposes in public and private herds in North America. Approximately 400,000 bison are owned by private individuals as livestock.

For our purposes in describing the bison's current range, let's stick with the major state and national parks where visitors are quite likely to observe them. The most logical place to begin is Yellowstone National Park in northwestern Wyoming.

Yellowstone National Park

In 1902 President Theodore Roosevelt appointed Charles "Buffalo" Jones as game warden in charge of Yellowstone's bison. Jones arranged for 21 bison (3 bulls and 18 cows) from private herds in Montana and Texas to supplement the approximately 30 bison

The Lamar Valley in Yellowstone National Park was home to some of the last surviving bison in the late 1800s.

remaining in Yellowstone. The bison population increased quickly, fluctuating dramatically over the next sixty-five years depending on prevailing management sentiments. In 1967 the park adopted a policy of limited management, where bison would range on their own without supplemental feed or significant management. The bison population in Yellowstone currently fluctuates between around 2,300 to 4,500 animals, depending on such factors as drought and winter severity.

Antelope Island

Antelope Island is the largest island in Utah's Great Salt Lake. In 1893 two Utah residents, John Dooley and William Glassman, transported 12 bison to the island by boat. The descendants of these bison are now managed to maintain a population of around 550 animals. A bison roundup occurs on the island each fall, when excess animals are sold at an auction. Limited sport hunting is also used to control the island's buffalo numbers.

The Wichita Mountains National Wildlife Refuge

In 1905 the Wichita Forest and Game Preserve was created in Oklahoma (later renamed the Wichita Mountains National Wildlife Refuge). Naturalist William Hornaday personally selected 15 bison from the New York Zoological Park to establish a buffalo herd here in 1907. By 1923 the herd had increased to nearly 150 animals. The bison population is currently maintained at about 650 animals on this 59,000-acre refuge in the southwestern portion of Oklahoma.

The National Bison Range

The National Bison Range in western Montana was established specifically for bison preservation. Created in 1908, this 18,500-acre refuge was originally stocked with 36 animals from the Conrad Kalispell herd in Montana. Four more bison were added from other private sources in its first year of operation. The herd grew rapidly, expanding to around 700 animals by 1924. To add genetic diversity, bison from other areas have been added to the herd at various times since its creation. The US Fish and Wildlife

The National Bison Range in western Montana was established specifically for the restoration of bison.

Service (USFWS) administers the National Bison Range. Bison are currently maintained at a level of around 350 animals.

The Fort Niobrara National Wildlife Refuge

The Fort Niobrara National Wildlife Refuge was created in 1912 by an executive order of President Theodore Roosevelt "as a preserve and breeding ground for native birds." Its mission soon expanded to the preservation of bison. In 1913 a private rancher in Nebraska gifted 6 bison to the refuge. Yellowstone National Park sent 2 more. A few bulls from the National Bison Range and Custer State Park were added on at least three occasions to limit inbreeding. This 19,131-acre refuge in north-central Nebraska maintains its bison herd at approximately 350 animals.

Custer State Park

Custer State Park in western South Dakota also became home to bison in 1913. The State of South Dakota purchased 36 bison from a private ranch and released them into the park. Since that time, Custer State Park has grown in size and now sprawls over 71,000 acres of grassland and low mountain (Black Hills) habitat that is ideal for bison. Around 1,300 bison roam the park, with the population varying somewhat depending on conditions. The herd is checked from overpopulation by culling excess animals through an auction sale and limited sport hunting.

Wind Cave National Park

In 1913 yet a third public bison herd was established, this one at Wind Cave National Park in western South Dakota. The New York Zoological Society donated 14 bison to create this herd, supplemented by another 6 animals from Yellowstone National Park in 1916. In the 1950s bison from Wind Cave were baited into Custer State Park, which adjoins the national park to the north. At about the same time, brucellosis, a disease harmful to domestic cattle, was discovered in the Wind Cave bison herd. For the next several decades, park management worked to eradicate the disease. The herd was declared brucellosis free by the State of South Dakota in 1986. Currently about 400 buffalo range across Wind Cave National Park. The herd size fluctuates due to natural conditions and culling of excess animals when numbers exceed the carrying capacity of the range.

The Henry Mountains

Along with Yellowstone National Park, the bison in the Henry Mountains of southeastern Utah are a truly free-ranging herd. The animals roam across approximately 300,000 acres. The federal government and the State of Utah administer more than 98 percent of the land the animals inhabit; private individuals own about 1.5 percent.

In 1941, 18 bison (3 bulls, 15 cows) were transplanted from Yellowstone National Park to the Henry Mountains. Another 5 bulls were relocated the following year. Since that time, no further additions have been made to the Henry Mountain herd. Disease (brucellosis) was discovered in the bison in 1962. The following year an extensive corralling operation was undertaken to test the bison for brucellosis and cull infected animals. As a result of their experience with the capture, the bison shifted their range. Prior to the 1963 capture, the buffalo used the Burr Desert as winter range and the Henry Mountains as summer range. Since that time, the bison have maintained a home range in the Henry Mountains. The Henry Mountain herd fluctuates in size from around 200 to over 400 animals. Sport hunting is the primary mechanism for population control. The Utah Division of Wildlife Resources manages the Henry Mountain bison.

Grand Teton National Park

Twenty bison were relocated from Yellowstone National Park to Grand Teton National Park in Wyoming in 1948. Disease in the herd hampered the struggling population, which was augmented by 12 bison from Theodore Roosevelt National Park in 1964. Prior to 1969 the buffalo were kept in a large enclosure. After being released from the enclosure to become free ranging, the bison herd expanded. At the present time around 600 bison live in Grand Teton National Park. The bison winter primarily on the nearby National Elk Refuge, where they receive supplemental feed, along with elk.

Theodore Roosevelt National Park

Theodore Roosevelt National Park in western North Dakota was originally established as a national monument in 1947 and consists of two separate areas, the North Unit and the South Unit. Bison were transplanted from the Fort Niobrara National Wildlife Refuge to the South Unit in 1956. The 29 bison reproduced rapidly in this prairie environment. In 1962, 20 bison were moved from the South Unit of the park to populate the North Unit. Due to their health and reproductive success in this excellent bison habitat, the herds are culled periodically to avoid overpopulation.

Theodore Roosevelt National Park in North Dakota provides excellent habitat for several hundred bison, like this massive bull.

Excess animals are sent to zoos, other national parks, and Native American tribes. The buffalo herd in the North Unit is maintained at 150 to 250 animals, the larger South Unit is managed for 200 to 500 animals, depending on range conditions.

Badlands National Park

South Dakota's Badlands National Park received 50 bison from Theodore Roosevelt National Park and 3 from the Fort Niobrara National Wildlife Refuge in 1963. Twenty additional bison from the Colorado National Monument joined the herd in 1983 as part of the decision to remove bison from the national monument. Centered in the bison's historic plains environment, the animals thrive in Badlands National Park. The herd generally grows at a rate of 15 percent or slightly more each year. Excess animals are culled as necessary to avoid overpopulation. The herd is managed to stay below the 600-animal carrying capacity of the park, although numbers occasionally exceed this target.

Caprocks State Park

In 1878, at the urging of his wife, a Texas cattleman name Charles Goodnight captured 2 bison calves. He added a few more in

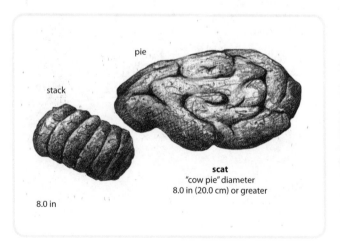

pie

stack

scat
"cow pie" diameter
8.0 in (20.0 cm) or greater

8.0 in

subsequent years, establishing a bison herd with seed stock from wild bison from the southern portion of the animals' native range. The herd grew to 125 animals by 1910 and to over 200 animals by 1920, its peak population. Stock from the Goodnight bison herd was used to populate several other public and private herds. After Goodnight's death his buffalo were sold several times. In 1997 the State of Texas took ownership of this genetically isolated bison herd and relocated them to Caprocks State Park. The herd has grown considerably from the 36 animals that came to the park.

Bison Habitat

Hoofed mammals fall along a continuum between species that are "grazers" and those that are "browsers." Grazers eat grass and other leafy plants; browsers eat plant material from trees and

Buffalo normally receive over 95 percent of their nutrition from grazing.

WHAT IS A "WILD" BISON?

Bison are one of the few mammals in North America that have dual status as wild animals and livestock. But the distinctions that help categorize similar species don't always apply as well to bison. For example, elk can be kept in private herds in some states. Other states, such as Montana, have banned any type of elk "farming." Farmed elk are commonly kept for meat or hunting. But most big-game hunters recognize that a "hunt" for elk kept in a private herd is much different than pursuing the truly wild animals that range across public lands in the West and some locations in eastern states. The animals on elk farms or private hunting clubs are kept in fenced enclosures, often fed supplemental feed, and are generally far more accustomed to humans than their free-ranging counterparts. Few observers would argue that they are wild elk.

Categorizing bison as "wild" or "domestic" is much more difficult. Most public bison herds are found in national parks, state parks, or national wildlife refuges that are enclosed with bison-proof fencing to keep the animals from wandering onto adjacent private or public lands. Is any animal contained by a fence truly wild? Most people believe that bison kept in huge enclosures such as those on the National Bison Range are wild. But what about smaller refuges where bison might range over a much smaller area of just a few hundred acres? Additionally, bison found on some private buffalo ranches roam across extensive tracts of land and behave similarly to those found in places like Custer State Park in South Dakota. Are they wild?

In a few places these questions don't apply. Bison in Yellowstone National Park in Wyoming, the Henry Mountains in Utah, and Wood Buffalo National Park in Alberta are not confined by fences. These animals are truly wild in every sense of the word. Elsewhere, it seems that categorizing bison as wild or livestock depends on the observer's perspective.

In the winter bison move snow with their massive heads to reach the grass underneath.

shrubs. Some animals, like elk, graze on grasses and other leafy plants, but they also browse on trees and shrubs.

Bison are grazing animals. Research indicates that bison do browse in some places, but browsing seldom exceeds 5 percent of their annual diet. In certain locations, however, bison do sometimes browse. In the Lamar Valley in Yellowstone National Park, researchers have discovered that bison frequently browse on willows along the Lamar River, both in the summer and the winter.

However, the bulk of the bison's diet comes from grasses and sedges (narrow-leafed plants similar to grass or rushes). As such, bison are found in habitats that support various species of grasses. Historically, the open grasslands of the central portion of North America were the finest bison habitat on the continent. However, bison were also found in remote mountain valleys and along river bottoms in the West. They roamed woodlands in the East, in areas where there was enough grasslike forage to maintain them.

In the Henry Mountains in Utah, bison range up to 11,000 feet in search of subalpine grasses in the summer. Bison are also found in high mountain valleys and along elevated ridges in Yellowstone National Park. Their massive size and thick coats make them very winter hardy and able to withstand cold temperatures. As such, they can winter in harsh environments, as long as there is grass to eat. Bison forage in the winter by moving snow with their massive heads to reach the grass underneath.

Chapter 3 Abilities and Behavior

Physical Abilities

The bison's large size and awkward-appearing shape betray an animal that is deceptively agile and swift. A bull bison can accelerate a ton of flesh and bones from a standing position to 30 miles per hour in a matter of seconds.

In 1986 a rodeo contestant and animal trainer named TC Thorstenson brought a trained bull bison to a horse race at a track in Gillette, Wyoming. The 2,700-pound bison swept the field by 2.5 lengths, easily winning a race spawned by a bet between parties debating the speed of a bison versus a horse. "Harvey Wallbanger," the male bison, was subsequently entered in numerous exhibition races around the United States, winning seventy-six of ninety-two contests against racehorses. Although he certainly wasn't competing against the top racehorses in the nation, his record amply illustrates the speed of a buffalo.

In the days when American Indians hunted bison with bow and arrow on horseback, hunters mounted themselves on "buffalo runners." Buffalo runners were horses that were exceptionally swift, sure-footed, and courageous. Only the Indians' finest mustangs could capably match the speed and maneuverability of a fleeing bison. While the native hunters usually aspired to kill more than one bison as they followed a herd dashing across the prairie, very few of their horses had the speed and endurance to run down more than one bison in a single chase, although historical records indicate Indian hunters sometimes killed two or three. Not only are bison fast, they can carry their speed for considerable distances. Observe a massive bull bison closely, and it's possible to detect some hint of its endurance. The hindquarters of the animal are narrow and lean. Disguised by the long hair descending from its front quarters, the shoulders power forelegs that are actually quite long. These physical features give bison a long stride that carries them efficiently across the prairie at high speeds.

Along with their straight-ahead speed, bison are very athletic in other ways. Bull bison have been observed jumping 6 feet from a standing position to clear obstacles. Cattle guards, a series of parallel poles or pipes set in a roadway a few inches apart, are often used to keep domestic livestock in a pasture. They are placed above a shallow pit where fences intersect a roadway, making it possible for cars to pass over, but prohibiting wandering cows to cross. Cattle guards are usually about 8 feet wide. In the case of bison, it takes a much wider cattle guard to check their movements. Bull bison are known to simply hop across an 8-foot cattle guard, clearing a span of some 14 feet considering that a bull bison is about 6 feet long.

When American Indians hunted bison on horseback and in current-day roundups, much of the danger involved stems from the buffalo's agility. These animals can change direction in the blink of an eye. When this happens, the mounted pursuer is in grave danger if the bison attempts to gore the pursuing horse. The amazing maneuverability of a bison comes from its physical structure. Much of its weight is centered over its front hooves, allowing it to pivot quickly without moving an extended amount of its mass. Bison also have specialized vertebrae above their shoulders with blades of bone that extend about a foot above their spine. These bones attach to large muscles and a tendon that extends to the base of the skull, allowing their massive head to turn very quickly and with considerable force.

Normally, however, bison go about their living at a slow plod. They move quite leisurely when grazing and spend long periods of time laying down, chewing their cud, and digesting their food. Herds of bison tend to travel at a measured pace, whether feeding during the cool hours of a summer day or moving from one snowy pasture to another in the winter. Biologists believe the unhurried movements of buffalo help them maximize their energy efficiency. Moving such a large body at high speeds requires burning a considerable amount of calories. The normally slow pace of a bison helps it conserve energy.

Along with their speed and agility, bison are also good swimmers. They are known to regularly swim across rivers spanning a half a mile or more. Researchers studying wood bison in Canada's Northwest Territories concluded that bison can also handle swift currents. Wood buffalo were observed swimming in currents with speeds up to 10 miles per hour without difficulty. In some areas, however, drowning is a significant source of bison mortality. Along the Liard River, a large stream in the Northwest

Bison are very comfortable in water and are good swimmers.

Territories in the Nahanni area, bison commonly swim to forage on both sides or on islands within the river. Animals may be swept away and drowned attempting to cross the river or from the islands when the river rises rapidly. This most often occurs in the spring, when snowmelt raises the river to its flood stage.

When swimming, bison calves and bulls sink low in the water. Some biologists speculate that this makes them more vulnerable to wave action or strong currents. Bison calves are sometimes drowned or swept downstream and abandoned by their mothers shortly after birth in areas where bison herds range on both sides of streams. In Yellowstone National Park buffalo congregate in the Lamar Valley at calving time. The Lamar River is easily waded by bison in midsummer, but can become a raging torrent due to snowmelt in the spring. Buffalo herds in the valley cross the river frequently. It is not unusual for a few calves to be swept away from their mothers when swimming the river at flood stage, sometimes drowning. At other times they wind up on islands in the river or in isolated areas downstream. These unattended calves are often discovered by predators such as grizzly bears, black bears, and wolves and are easy prey. Occasionally, however, diligent female bison search the riverbanks and are reunited with their flushed away calves.

Vocal and Visual Communication

Bison lack the range of vocal communication observed in canine predators, such as wolves and coyotes. However, at certain seasons within the yearly life cycle, bison are quite noisy. After calves are born in the spring, mothers and babies often maintain contact vocally. The basic call between cows and calves is a grunt that sounds somewhat similar to the grunting of a domestic hog. Cows and calves also grunt occasionally when grazing, a call that has a contented tone. The frequency of their communication increases when a herd is on the move in search of better grass or on the way to water. After a herd has stampeded, a period of intense, more frantic grunting often ensues, as if the cows and calves are saying to one another, "Here I am. Where are you?"

Once separated, cows and calves use their grunt calls to get back together. Sometimes, however, they get fooled. A cow and calf may move toward one another from opposite sides of the herd, attracted by each other's voice. When they approach, they may sniff each other and then move away. Although their ears might mistake their grunt for that of another bison, their nose never lies. I have observed similar behavior in herds of domestic cattle during a roundup. Evidently the ears of cattle-like mammals aren't capable of perfectly discerning between the calls of different animals.

Bull bison become very vocal during the mating season, which occurs in late summer. Described as a "bellow" or "roar," bull bison breathe out a loud, rolling sound that announces their presence to rival bulls in the herd and the cows with which they wish to mate. On calm days the bellows of a bison bull can sometimes be heard from over a mile away. When many bulls are roaring in a large herd of buffalo, people who are not familiar with this peculiar noise may mistake the sound for the rumbling of thunder. When two bull bison are in conflict over a cow, their bellowing becomes more frequent and intense.

Along with vocalizations, bison communicate in other ways as well. They use body language, such as postures and movements that signal their "mood" and intentions to other buffalo, predators, or humans. When nursing, bison calves often vigorously wag their tails like a happy dog. This wagging appears to signal its pleasure, similar to a mutt having just received a treat. Bison cows sometimes nuzzle their nursing calves, a gesture that indicates the bond between a mother and her offspring. Cows are also known to rest their heads gently on the back of their calves and lick their calves, especially when they are very young.

Bison signal aggressive intentions in a variety of ways. Bulls have an elaborate series of behaviors they use to communicate aggression, dominance, or submission during the mating season, a subject we'll explore in Chapter 5. However, buffalo communicate agitation at other times during the year through

The bellow of a bull bison can sometimes be heard from a mile away.

several common behaviors. A raised tail is one of the most widespread signals of a defensive or aggressive attack. Bison also snort, stamp their feet, and shake their heads to communicate their displeasure. Where trees are present, they may also gore the trunk or branches with their horns. While one or more of these physical signals usually precedes aggressive activity, bison sometimes charge a perceived threat without any prior behavioral cue.

Herd Structure and Dynamics

Bison are gregarious animals that spend most of their lives in herds that may range in size from a half dozen to several hundred. Except during the mating season, cows and mature bulls are found in distinct herds. Cow herds are larger and more diverse than smaller bands of bulls. Cows, their most recently born calves, and adolescent animals of both sexes congregate in the cow herds.

The close bond between a mother bison and her calf persists until she no longer has milk for her offspring, at which time it is weaned. Weaning generally occurs around 7 or 8 months of age

A cow herd of bison moves toward better pasture in early spring. Cow herds are composed of cows, calves, and young bulls.

or shortly thereafter, a condition that is somewhat influenced by the availability of forage for the mother, her age, and body condition. After weaning, bison calves stay in the cow herd with their mothers but don't spend as much time in close proximity to them. By the time they are yearlings (1 year old), bison calves are essentially independent of their mothers, although they remain in the same herd. Female bison may remain in the same herd as their mother for many years, perhaps as long as both mother and daughter are alive. Bison bulls usually depart their mothers' cow herd at 3 to 4 years of age.

Once they leave the cow herd, bison bulls join groups of other males that form smaller bands than the cow herds. They remain in these bull herds or bachelor groups from fall to midsummer. During the mating season the bull herds splinter, with various males joining cow herds that share a similar range. Although bison cows are rarely found alone, bull bison may become solitary creatures. Many observers believe that lone bull bison are the older members of the male population, animals that may have been driven from a cow herd by dominant younger bulls and retained a solitary lifestyle afterward. In some cases lone bison bulls do not participate in the breeding season at all. I have observed large, single bison bulls apart from cow herds during the breeding season in several national parks.

Bison appear to form herds primarily for protection. Both bulls and cows participate in repelling a predatory threat from animals such as wolves. When confronted by predators, buffalo may form a defensive position around calves. Having multiple animals within a herd make it more likely that some member of the group will detect danger. If the herd flees, being a member of a large group increases the odds that any single animal will be targeted for predation.

There are dominance hierarchies within both bull and cow herds. Dominance hierarchies simply refer to the idea of a pecking order or a structure in which certain animals will yield to others during competition for food, water, mating, or other biological resources. Researchers have found that where forage is abundant, the dominance structure in cow herds revolves most predominantly around age. Cows that are 3 years old dominate those that are 2 years old. Cows that are 6 can push around those that are 4. Intense competition for food might disrupt this basic pattern, but otherwise cow bison tend to follow the idea of "respect your elders."

The situation is similar for bulls in their early years of life but changes as they grow older. Research on bison bulls kept in captivity indicates that some bulls may become capable of reproduction at around 1.5 years of age. However, most experts feel that wild bison bulls reach fertility at 2 to 3 years of age. Nonetheless, these younger bulls aren't normally able to reproduce until a few years later in life. Bulls in the 6- to 8-year-old

Some naturalists believe old bull bison are more likely to become loners than those in their prime. The stubby, worn horns of this solitary bull betray his advanced age.

Young bison are buffered from predators by the herd. Biologists believe bison form herds primarily for protection.

KING OF THE BOVINES?

Domestic cattle and bison belong to the bovine family of animals. Capable of interbreeding, the kinship between buffalo and cattle is clear. The males of both species are incredibly large, powerful animals. Which is king of the bovines, a 2,000-pound male bison or a massive domestic bull?

In 1907 a fight between an 8-year-old bull bison and a Mexican fighting bull was staged in Juarez, Mexico. A South Dakota rancher was visiting friends in El Paso, Texas. After watching a bullfight in Juarez, the American cattleman asserted that he knew of bulls back home that could easily best the Mexican champion. When the Mexican bull handlers found out he was referring to a bull bison, they were insulted. A $10,000 bet on a contest between a Mexican fighting bull and a bull bison resulted.

After a grueling seven-day journey from South Dakota to Juarez, two bison bulls arrived for the fight. When the older of the two was turned into the ring, it became apparent that he'd injured a hind leg in transport. Nonetheless, he easily repelled the charges of a Mexican bull with his massive head. After defeating the first sharp-horned Mexican bull, he handily dominated three others that were subsequently turned into the ring.

However, a similar incident in 1847 turned out differently. In this case a driver from Fort Union was hauling wood in a cart pulled by a domestic bull. Suddenly the pair was attacked by a bison bull blocking their path back to the fort. The ensuing battle was fierce, with the domestic bull finally killing the belligerent buffalo.

Centuries of domestication have changed the character of wild cattle to domestic cows. Yet within the large, awkward-looking bodies of domestic bulls sometimes lives the wild spirit of their ancestors. Be it a majestic bull bison or a hulking beef bull, only a fool takes for granted the raw power of these battering bovines.

range, or those slightly older, dominate the breeding hierarchy. One observational study in Yellowstone National Park concluded that bulls over the age of 8 years are most successful in mating. Once bulls reach their prime around age 6, they must rely on their strength, size, and fighting ability to maintain their rank in the bull herd and at breeding time.

Chapter 4 Bison and Other Animals

Bison and Predators

The list of predators in North America capable of killing bison is very short. Under normal circumstances only gray wolves and grizzly bears can successfully prey upon adult bison. Predation attempts by grizzly bears on adult animals are very rare. Black bears, mountain lions, and coyotes have the ability to kill bison in their first few months of life, but it would be highly abnormal for these predators to target an adult or even yearling bison.

The massive size of adult bison (especially bulls) makes them highly immune to most predators.

Bison and Wolves

When Europeans began regularly exploring the central portion of the United States in the late eighteenth and early nineteenth centuries, they encountered seemingly innumerable herds of bison. Along with buffalo they also observed gray wolves in great numbers. The predator-prey relationship between wolves and bison was recorded in the writings of numerous early explorers. On their epic journey to the Pacific Ocean, Lewis and Clark encountered "vast assemblages" of wolves. The explorers noted in their journals that large packs of wolves constantly accompanied the great herds of bison (and elk) they encountered along the Missouri River in Montana.

Other pioneering journalists noted more specific interactions between these bands of prey and predator. In 1834 Charles Joseph Latrobe, an English explorer and mountaineer, made an expedition through North America with Washington Irving. Latrobe observed wolves and bison in many areas, including present-day Oklahoma. He noted in his writings that wolves "hunt the straggling cows and calves in packs."

Historically, wolves were the primary predator of bison. Today, in places where they are both found, this historical relationship has reasserted itself. Its basic pattern is similar to what Latrobe recorded nearly two centuries ago. Wolves regularly kill bison in some areas, almost always targeting immature animals or females.

Where do wolves prey upon bison in modern times? In the United States Yellowstone and Grand Teton National Parks in northwestern Wyoming are the only places the two species frequently come into contact with one another. Both national parks are home to moose and elk, animals that wolves generally target for predation before attempting to bring down bison, which are larger and normally more difficult to kill. Biologists have recorded very few bison predation attempts by wolves in Grand Teton National Park, perhaps due to the relatively low number of bison and large number of elk that winter in the area.

In Yellowstone wolves have been observed killing bison since shortly after their reintroduction to the park in 1995. Although

Wolves regularly prey upon bison in some areas. Most of the bison killed by wolves are taken in the winter.

bison do not constitute a major portion of a wolf's diet within the park as a whole, in certain areas they are very important prey. On average, bison account for less than 5 percent of the gray wolf's prey in Yellowstone. However, in the central portion of the park from which elk migrate in the winter, bison are the wolf's major prey during the snowy months. Bison are also the most important prey for wolves in areas of northern Canada, most notably Wood Buffalo National Park and the Slave River Lowlands. In these areas bison may account for 80 to 90 percent of a wolf's annual diet.

In Alaska wolves sometimes kill bison. Due to the remote nature of much of the habitat occupied by Alaskan bison, little research has been done to document the extent to which they are preyed upon by wolves.

In places where wolves consistently prey on bison, biologists have recorded certain trends and behaviors in this fascinating interaction between predator and prey. For example, winter is the season when wolves bring down the majority of the bison. Other prey animals are more commonly available in the summer months, including other hoofed animals and smaller quarry such as birds and rodents. In Yellowstone National Park over 90 percent of the bison killed by wolves are taken in the winter. Buffalo brought down by wolves at other times of the year are typically young calves separated from their mothers or animals that have been injured.

The wolves of Yellowstone and northern Canada that routinely prey upon bison in the winter show a distinct preference for juvenile animals and cows. Unless injured or severely weakened by nutritional stress in late winter, bison bulls are too large and dangerous for wolves to attack. Wolves most commonly target animals that are enduring their first winter, but can also kill adult cows.

Successful predation of bison by wolves tends to follow a consistent pattern. A pack of wolves confronts a bison herd. In some areas they use trees or brush to conceal their approach, but they often move directly toward a bison herd without any attempts at stealth. The wolves then harass the herd, hoping to separate vulnerable animals from the band. When bison stand their ground, wolves most often abandon the attack unless they are extremely hungry. As pack members harass the buffalo with lunges and biting, the bison may panic and begin to run. When this occurs, the wolves follow in pursuit, targeting vulnerable animals from the rear, biting and holding their hind legs and flanks. Bison that are slowed or held by a wolf or two are then overcome by the rest of the pack. Wolves in the interior region of Yellowstone National Park often attempt to chase a bison herd

Young bison are more vulnerable to wolf predation. Immature animals separated from the herd are most easily taken by wolves.

into areas of deep snow, such as drifted ravines, where the entire pack can swarm upon a floundering buffalo.

Wolf packs that are consistently successful in killing bison have several characteristics in common. On the whole, wolf packs with higher numbers are more capable of killing bison than those with fewer hunters. Packs that regularly hunt bison often number ten or more wolves. Along with increased numbers, wolves that must bring down buffalo to survive are some of the largest of their kind in North America. Bison-eating wolves of northern Canada are notably big, as are their counterparts in Yellowstone. The largest wolves observed in Yellowstone most commonly belong to the packs that hunt bison in the winter. Additionally, these packs also contain more adult male wolves than usual. The central Yellowstone wolf pack that accounts for the most bison kills in the park frequently contains several large adult males. The superior size and strength of these wolves helps them bring down buffalo that may weigh ten times as much as any single wolf in the pack.

Bison and Grizzly Bears

Adult grizzly bears are capable of killing adult bison. However, grizzly bear predation on adult bison is very rare. In the fall of 2000, a park employee in Yellowstone National Park observed a female grizzly bear pursue a young adult bison that the bear startled at close range. When the bull buffalo ran, it was pursued and knocked from its feet by the bear. It then slid down a steep embankment and was repeatedly attacked by the bear. The bison was apparently injured when it slammed against a tree in the slide. The attack terminated in an area where the bear was driven from the badly wounded bison to protect the safety of park visitors and construction workers. Wildlife managers euthanized the bison. Experts believe the grizzly bear would have completed its predation in the absence of human interference.

Historical records indicate one other credible reference to a grizzly bear bringing down a cow bison. Circumstantial evidence in Alaska (grizzly bears discovered on adult bison

Grizzly bears occasionally prey upon young bison. Predation attempts on adult bison by grizzly bears are very rare, but they have been recorded.

carcasses) may also suggest that the grizzlies prey upon adult bison on rare occasions. Biologists believe that when grizzly bears do kill adult bison, it is most likely in late winter or early spring when hungry bears emerging from hibernation encounter buffalo that have been substantially weakened from malnutrition after a severe winter.

Bears don't frequently target bison calves, but grizzly bears have been observed killing bison in the first few months of life in Yellowstone National Park. When bison cows bunch together to protect their calves, they can normally repel the investigations of bears. However, if the herd stampedes or a grizzly bear discovers a lone cow and calf, the bear can successfully run down the young bison. Some evidence also exists of black bears killing very young bison calves. Nonetheless, bison predation by bears of either species is highly unusual.

Bison and Coyotes and Mountain Lions

Under similar circumstances, coyotes and mountain lions might successfully kill young bison calves. In one very unusual incident, several coyotes were observed assisting a wolf in killing a young bison. After the bison was brought down, the wolf chased the coyotes from the kill. Suffice it to say that wolves frequently prey upon bison in some places. Otherwise, bison mortality from predation is a very rare occurrence.

Bison and Other Herbivores

In an age before humans factored predominantly in the history of the bison in North America, these animals shared their habitat with a host of other plant-eating mammals. On the prairies where they were most numerous, bison lived alongside large herbivores such as elk, pronghorn, and eventually wild horses. However, they also interacted with smaller plant eaters, including many species of ground squirrels and prairie dogs.

Bison and Elk

Although the diets of elk, bison, and pronghorn overlap somewhat, the species do not compete directly for food. Bison and elk are occasionally viewed in proximity to one another, but if their paths cross directly, elk yield to bison. Elk graze more than deer or pronghorn, giving them more dietary overlap with bison. Biologists at the National Bison Range have historically considered elk as equivalent to .70 bison, deer as .40 bison, and pronghorn as .25 bison in relation to forage consumption in that area. In a few areas bison might impact elk browsing on willows and other deciduous plants commonly consumed by elk in the winter. However, most biologists believe that competition between elk and bison for forage is not a limiting factor in local populations of either animal.

In some places elk may buffer bison from wolf predation. Where elk and bison are both available prey to wolves, the

When both species are available, wolves prefer to prey on elk rather than bison. An abundant elk population may buffer bison from predation.

canines prefer elk. In the years since wolves were reintroduced to Yellowstone National Park, bison numbers have increased on the northern range, an area once heavily populated by elk. Some researchers believe wolf predation on elk has improved overall habitat conditions for both elk and bison in terms of available forage. With wolves targeting elk far more often than bison, more buffalo than elk are allowed to take advantage of the improved range conditions.

Bison and Prairie Dogs

It is estimated that millions and millions of bison once roamed the Great Plains. How many prairie dogs do you suppose tunneled into the sod beneath them? If the thought of thirty million bison taxes your brain, what about five billion prairie dogs? That's exactly how many of these rodents some biologists believe once lived in

Although they may weigh less than 1/1,000th of an adult bison, prairie dogs are actually beneficial to bison.

North America. Although they only weigh about 1.5 pounds, the astronomical number of prairie dogs made them an animal that had considerable impact on prairie ecosystems. Prairie dogs were an important food source for countless predators including foxes, coyotes, black-footed ferrets, eagles, hawks, and rattlesnakes.

Bison and prairie dogs historically existed in a mutually beneficial relationship that persists today in places like Custer State Park, Badlands National Park, and Theodore Roosevelt National Park in the Dakotas. Prairie dogs do not exist in tall grass. Instead, the rodents and bison feed on the grass in a prairie dog town (a place where many prairie dogs live together in an extended colony), keeping it short. Bison are attracted to prairie dog towns by the tender new shoots that arise from the closely cropped grass in the spring or after rainfall in the summer. Feeding bison keep the grass from growing too tall for the prairie dogs. Their dung and urine add nutrients to the dirt around the prairie dog town, enhancing the productivity of the soil. In an odd twist of ecology, one of the prairie's largest mammals benefits from a small, burrowing rodent.

Parasites and Diseases

Bison and cattle share many common parasites and diseases. However, due to their physiological differences, infection rates and physical symptoms of parasites and diseases are not always similar in the two species, even where they share habitat. Research in the Henry Mountains in Utah has shown that even where they occupy the same range, the parasite prevalence between buffalo and cattle is different.

The exposure of bison in public herds to parasites and diseases depends on where they live. Bison of the far north in places such as Canada's Wood Buffalo National Park may be exposed to very different parasites and diseases than those roaming the Wichita Mountains National Wildlife Refuge in Oklahoma. Because much of the bison research involving parasites and disease has been conducted in private herds, it is difficult to establish with certainty the extent to which animals in public herds might be affected.

Internal parasites that are known to afflict bison include lungworms and tapeworms. These parasites are not normally a significant cause of bison mortality, but they may weaken or kill individual animals that are severely infected. Bison are also sometimes plagued by a variety of external parasites, such as mosquitoes, ticks, and biting flies. The long, dense hair of bison makes it difficult for ticks to reach their skin. Bison also roll in the dirt (wallow) and groom themselves by scratching with their hind feet or rubbing on trees and rocks. Both activities help dislodge ticks from the body. When their coat is short during the summer months, bison are sometimes harassed by biting flies to the point that they abandon feeding areas where fly infestations are

Rubbing on trees and rocks helps bison rid themselves of ticks and other external parasites.

particularly acute. Some researchers believe bison found at very high elevations in the summer may be avoiding biting insects more prevalent at lower elevations.

Bison are susceptible to a number of diseases that are also found in domestic cattle. Domestic animals such as cattle and sheep may transmit certain diseases to bison and vice versa.

Brucellosis is a disease common to bison in Yellowstone National Park. Brucellosis is caused by bacteria of the *brucella* family and can infect a variety of animals including cattle, bison, elk, goats, pigs, camels, dogs, and humans. Bison are affected by the strain known as *brucella abortus*. As the name implies, severe brucellosis may cause a female buffalo to abort her fetus. Other symptoms of brucellosis include swollen joints and testicles, infertility, lameness, and reduced milk production. In most cases, however, bison that are infected with the bacteria do not exhibit readily observable symptoms of the disease.

Over the past century the livestock industry has spent considerable resources to eradicate brucellosis from domestic livestock. Brucellosis is of concern to ranchers due to its economics. Aborted fetuses cost ranchers calves. The disease also requires ranchers to spend money on testing and vaccinations, and it causes weight loss and other factors that adversely affect cattle production.

The potential for bison to transmit brucellosis to cattle in areas adjacent to Yellowstone National Park is a very contentious political and economic issue. Some groups believe Yellowstone bison should be allowed to migrate to adjacent public lands without interference. Others believe the bison should be kept away from area cattle even if it requires lethal control. At the present time the State of Montana uses hunting as a means to control bison that wander beyond the boundaries of the park. Hunters take the animals for meat, but the state also hopes to keep bison from mingling with cattle by hunting them.

Bovine tuberculosis is another bacterial disease that is sometimes found in bison. The disease causes lesions in the lungs and lymph nodes and may be fatal to infected animals. Outbreaks

BRUCELLOSIS AND THE ELK INTERFACE

It is widely recognized that the area in and around Yellowstone National Park (commonly known as the Greater Yellowstone Ecosystem, or GYE) is the last remaining reservoir of brucellosis in the United States. Various proposals to limit the exposure of cattle to the disease in the area often concentrate on the potential transmission from bison to cattle. As such, some have advocated a brucellosis eradication program within the park's bison herd. In domestic cattle such programs involve the monitoring of the disease in a herd, vaccination, and elimination of infected animals. Such a procedure is potentially possible with Yellowstone's bison and has been successfully employed in other public bison herds. However, buffalo aren't as easy to capture and handle as cattle, and the prospect of killing animals that test positive for the disease raises the hackles of many environmental groups, not to mention their resistance to the hazing and handling of these wild animals.

As long as elk are part of the landscape, such a program may be futile anyway. Elk harbor brucellosis along with bison. They range over a greater portion of the GYE and aren't so easy to monitor. The extent to which the disease is mobile among elk, bison, and cattle isn't clearly understood. However, it appears possible that even if brucellosis were eradicated within bison of the GYE, if the disease wasn't also purged from elk, the bison could later become re-infected. All parties seem to agree that eradicating brucellosis (a disease that was probably brought to the United States from Europe and possibly introduced to the Yellowstone area by cattle) from Yellowstone's bison (and elk) would solve a host of problems. The questions of "if" and "how" it can be accomplished aren't as easy to answer.

of bovine tuberculosis have occurred in various public and private bison herds during the past century. Research indicates that some bison inhabiting Wood Buffalo National Park are infected with both bovine tuberculosis and brucellosis.

Anthrax is another bacterial disease known to occasionally infect public bison herds in North America. Bison may also be susceptible to other bacterial and viral infections found in cattle and other ungulates.

Chapter 5

Reproduction and Young

The Mating Season

Bison calves are born in the spring, but the reproductive cycle of these massive grazers actually begins the previous summer. The bison mating season occurs in midsummer, usually spanning the weeks of late July and early August. Cows that do not conceive a calf during the normal breeding season may mate a month or so later. Within some bison herds half of the cows may become pregnant in the span of a week.

As the breeding season approaches, the bachelor herds of mature bulls splinter. Bulls join the cow herds, moving through

During the breeding season bulls in the prime of life patrol the cow herds in search of cows that are ready to mate.

This bison bull is "tending" the cow, keeping himself between her and potential rivals in the herd.

the females in search of cows that are preparing to breed. Throughout the rest of the year, the massive males live together with very little conflict, resting and grazing in their bull groups. During the mating season, however, bulls that have achieved sufficient size and status in the herd to claim cows find themselves in competition with other males.

Public bison herds from which animals are not culled often have a nearly equal number of breeding-age bulls and cows. The majority of the cows become ready for breeding in a short span of time, creating intense competition among the mature bulls. Shortly before a cow is ready for breeding, she is joined by a "tending" bull. The bull often attempts to separate the cow a short distance from the herd or keeps her at the edge of the buffalo band. He positions his body between the cow and rival bulls, communicating his intention to mate with the cow to both the female and other competitive males. This tending behavior persists for several hours until the cow is bred or a rival bull drives the bull from the cow. In some cases the cow breaks from a tending bull and bolts back into the herd, apparently attempting to motivate the advances of a bull that is superior to the one courting her.

Two dramatic displays of bison athletics occur during the breeding season, one that involves cows, another that takes place between bulls. While it's easy to assume that the big, bold bison bulls are the fastest animals in the herd, it's the cows that are swiftest of feet and more agile. If a cow isn't sufficiently impressed with the bull tending her, she may attempt to dash away from him. Bulls respond to these maneuvers by their own rushes as they try to keep themselves between the cow and potential rivals. This action appears very similar to the activities of a cowboy on horseback who uses his mount to cut a cow away from the herd for roping. Many biologists believe that bison cows are nearly always capable of escaping a tending bull. A cow's attempts to evade him might simply be part of her assessment of a bull's desirability as the sire of her calf. If a cow really decides to escape from a tending bull, her speed and agility are impressive. Equally inspiring is the number of rival bulls that come rushing from the herd to claim her.

Most of the conflict between bulls during the mating season is settled with aggressive displays that result in one bull backing down from another when they contest the breeding privileges of a cow. Confronted with an older, larger bull, a young male just coming into breeding age is most likely to back away without a contest. Mature bulls that are evenly matched in size and rank within the herd aren't so easily intimidated. Whether challenging one another over a receptive cow or jostling for dominance in the breeding hierarchy, bulls of roughly equal stature engage in a variety of threatening behaviors intended to intimidate their rivals into submission. The vocal aspect of the threat involves bellowing. As a bull approaches a rival, his bellows usually become louder, more frequent, and more intense. However, one university research study on the Fort Niobrara National Wildlife Refuge in Nebraska found that the volume of a bull's bellows was inversely correlated to his breeding success. The truly dominant animals seemed to adopt more of a policy of "walk softly but carry a big stick" than their loudmouthed rivals.

Along with the vocal menace, a threatening bull relies on a number of physical behaviors to communicate his intentions. Bulls stomp their feet as they walk toward a rival. They also urinate in a wallow (a patch of bare ground where bison roll in the dust to relieve itching or rid themselves of insects), then wallow in the damp soil. Some biologists believe this seemingly random act gives rival bulls some indication of a male's fitness that can be detected by his opponent's keen sense of smell.

If the threats of bellowing, stomping, and wallowing don't resolve the conflict, bulls engage in a series of closer postures that may lead them to a full-blown battle. Bulls may approach each other directly with their heads cocked slightly to one side. If one of the animals turns aside, he is admitting the dominance of his rival. They may also confront one another from a parallel position with their bodies broadside to one another. The confrontation may also lead to the two hulking males coming nearly within touching distance of each other, then simultaneously bobbing their heads in a threatening manner.

When none of these threats or postures successfully intimidates a rival, a battle ensues. The confrontation begins with the butting of heads or one bull attempting to hook the other with his short, pointed horns. Some fights are momentary, ending when one bull signals his submission by turning his head sideways and backing away between clashes. Others are lengthy tests of strength and courage that end with the injury of one or both bulls. Fighting bison repeatedly clash their massive heads together, pivoting swiftly about on their front feet in an attempt to reach their opponent's ribcage or flank. If a bull is successful

Rival bulls use wallowing in the dirt as a threatening signal during the mating season.

Full-blown fights between mature bull bison often begin as head-to-head confrontations. When one bull attempts to hook the other with a horn or rams his head, the battle begins.

in pressing such an attack, he may gore his rival in the ribs, abdomen, or hindquarters. Ribs may be broken when this occurs, or the horn of one bull may pierce the hide of another. Legs may be fractured or joints dislocated as well. In rare instances a bison bull may kill his opponent on the spot. More frequently, bulls die from infected puncture wounds or injuries that make them unable to travel and feed.

Bison bulls may lose over 10 percent of their body weight (sometimes over 200 pounds) during the breeding season. The weight loss stems from calories burned during stressful threatening displays and fighting. During the mating season bull bison spend more of their time confronting rivals and mating, and less time eating. Their lower nutritional intake and high output during this time may cause dominant bulls to lose so much weight that they are at increased risk of starvation in a severe winter.

Pregnancy and Gestation

In bison herds that have access to highly nutritious forage on a consistent basis, as many as 90 percent of the mature cows may conceive a calf. Conception rates in public herds that do not receive supplemental feed are more variable. Drought, winter severity, and other environmental factors affect the percentage of cows that bear calves in the spring. Historical records from Yellowstone National Park from 1931 to 1966 show pregnancy rates that fluctuate from around 50 to 90 percent depending on the year. Other public bison herds have experienced pregnancy rates as low as 35 percent in times of nutritional stress.

Bison females are most reproductively successful from around 4 to 12 years of age. Older cows occupying good habitat frequently birth calves as well. One cow on the Wichita Mountains National Wildlife Refuge in Oklahoma lived to be 31 years old and raised a calf at age 28. Other females in the Wichita Mountains herd have birthed calves beyond age 20. However, calving rates appear to decline sharply in females over 15 years old.

The gestation period (the time between conception and birth) for bison is similar to that of domestic cattle and slightly longer than humans. The most commonly reported gestation length for bison is 9.5 months or 285 days. Various scientific studies indicate that gestation may vary from 270 to 300 days. Within 6 months of pregnancy, a bison fetus weighs around 25 to 30 pounds, or about 60 percent of its birth weight. The last 3 months of gestation result in the most rapid growth of the unborn bison calf.

Birth

Under natural conditions most bison calves are born between late April and early June. The calving season can be manipulated in buffalo herds kept as livestock. Both the timing and duration of the birthing period vary somewhat by region. Research at the National Bison Range in western Montana has recorded as high as 97 percent of the births occurring in a three-week period from the last week in April to the second week in May. Researchers have observed a significantly longer calving period at Wind Cave

National Park in South Dakota and the Fort Niobrara National Wildlife Refuge in Nebraska. A small percentage of bison calves may be born later in the summer.

The high concentration of bison births in a short period of time is part of a biological phenomenon known as "synchronous breeding." Young bison calves, like other newborn ungulates, are much more vulnerable to predation in the first few weeks of life than they are later in the summer. Evolutionary biologists theorize that synchronous breeding increases the odds of some bison calves achieving an age at which they're less susceptible to predation. When predators encounter such a large number of potential prey, "predator satiation" occurs, making it more likely that some of the prey will survive.

Birthing normally occurs on the bison's winter range. Individual cows leave the herd to birth their calves in solitude, rejoining the maternal band a short time later. The birthing process lasts but a few minutes, with the cow usually lying down but sometimes standing. The mother vigorously assists the newborn in freeing itself from the birthing membranes and urges it to its feet with licks and nuzzling. Calves normally attempt to stand just a few minutes after birth and can move in a clumsy run within an hour. For the first few days of life, the calf spends most of its time lying down, standing to nurse. Bison females do not produce as much milk as a domestic cow, but it is incredibly rich.

Newborn bison are very similar in appearance to newborn domestic calves, lacking the hump of their parents that will develop within a few months. The brick red or cinnamon color of the bison calf also transitions in its first months of life to the dark brown of an adult. Baby bison weigh around forty to fifty pounds at birth, with birth weights varying noticeably in some locations. Average birth weights at the Fort Niobrara National Wildlife Refuge in Nebraska are reported at fifty to sixty pounds. Newborn bison on Antelope Island in Utah average twenty-five to forty pounds. Bison cows normally birth a single offspring. Twin bison calves are quite rare.

Young bison calves are similar in appearance to the offspring of domestic cattle, lacking the characteristic hump, horns, and coloration of their parents.

BISON MILK FOR BREAKFAST?

Americans most commonly drink the milk of domestic cows. In some places goat milk is also available. In other parts of the world, humans receive nutrition from the milk of many other species of animals. Visiting a "supermarket" in Mongolia several years ago, I was intrigued to find horse and camel milk available, along with milk from cows and goats. Yaks, a relative of bison and domestic cows, are milked in some places.

So, why not bison milk? In the first place milking a bison cow is no easy task. Bison may be kept as livestock, but they are never tamed. Milking a bison cow means confining it in a special apparatus known as a squeeze chute. The process is not pleasant for the kicking cow, nor the enterprising person doing the milking.

However, reports indicate that early bison keepers at the National Bison Range in Montana and elsewhere occasionally milked bison cows. For some time newcomers to bison tending at the the National Bison Range drank bison milk as part of an informal ritual. Some liked the taste; others did not. A test of bison milk in Oklahoma reputedly indicated that it was much richer than that of a Jersey cow, one of the breeds of domestic dairy cows known for exceptionally rich milk. Although a few humans probably taste milk from bison cows kept in private herds each year, it's not something you'll soon be able to add to your cereal for breakfast!

Nurturing Calves to Adulthood

On the whole, bison cows are very attentive mothers, although in rare instances they may abandon their newborn calf. A few days after birth, the cow rejoins the cow herd with her young calf. Although cows within the herd care for their individual calves, the young buffalo also receives the protection and care of the entire maternal herd. Bison cows have been observed banding together to repel predators. In a unique instance in Yellowstone National Park, a cow was photographed deliberately nudging a group of calves to their feet during very cold, snowy weather in early May, reducing their chances of freezing to death.

Some research indicates female calves remain with their mothers longer than male calves. In either case bison calves can survive in the herd without direct maternal care by their first winter.

Bison calves nurse for about the first seven or eight months of life, sometimes a bit longer. Bison calves have been observed attempting to graze within a week of birth and will drink water after their first week. Once weaned from mother's milk, a young bison stays in the cow herd of its mother, but the close association between female and offspring begins to fade. Some research indicates that female calves remain in closer proximity to their mothers within the herd for a much longer period after weaning than male offspring. In either case young bison are able to forage and survive within the herd after weaning.

Chapter 6 Bison and Humans

Bison in Prehistoric Times

The bison of the current era were preceded by several related species. Although imposing animals, modern bison are actually smaller than their predecessors. The first bison in North America are believed to have been Steppe bison or Ice Age bison (*Bison priscus*), which arrived on the continent from Siberia.

In a fascinating twist of history, miners discovered a frozen intact carcass of a Steppe bison near Fairbanks, Alaska, in 1979. The animal was a mature bull, perhaps 8 or 9 years old, that had been killed by American lions, large cats similar to today's African lions that once roamed North America. Radiocarbon dating indicates that the bison was killed some 36,000 years ago. Its death came in late fall or early winter. The lions fed on the animal's hump and flesh that covered the ribs on one side, but scientists believe the carcass froze shortly thereafter. They theorize the bison remained frozen and inhospitable to scavengers during the winter and was perhaps covered by a mudslide in the spring. It then became entombed in the permafrost, remaining in remarkably good condition until it was exposed by the miners. A reaction between chemicals in the bison's tissue and minerals in the surrounding soil created a compound that produced a bright blue color when exposed to the air. This phenomenon earned the bull the nickname "Blue Babe," in reference to the mythical Paul Bunyan's blue ox.

The horns of Steppe bison were much longer than those of today's bison, but a later species that descended from the Steppe bison sported even longer horns that sometimes spanned more than 6 feet from tip to tip. Sometimes called Giant Ice Age bison (*Bison latifrons*), these giant creatures were 20 to 25 percent larger than today's bison. Bulls would have weighed nearly 3,000 pounds, with exceptionally large specimens possibly exceeding 1.5 tons by a few hundred pounds. Both of these species became

This postage stamp from Romania was issued in 1966. It shows images of an Ice Age bison (*Bison priscus*).

extinct some 10,000 years ago. Several smaller-bodied, smaller-horned descendants of these bison also ranged across portions of North America. But by the time the first Europeans set foot on the continent and the native peoples acquired horses, only the American bison (*Bison bison*) remained.

Bison and American Indians

The vast herds of buffalo on the central grasslands in North America nurtured human cultures intimately tied to their presence. Some historians believe that the connection between the plains tribes of American Indians and bison illustrates the strongest dependence on one animal by any human society from prehistoric times to the present. Bison provided these native peoples with food (meat), shelter (hides), and tools (bone, sinew, and other body parts). Red Cloud, a former chief of the Sioux tribe, purportedly listed twenty-two uses of the bison by his people. Others have placed the number as high as eighty-seven.

American Indians hunted the vast herds of bison on the plains and foothills of the Rocky Mountains for thousands of years before they acquired horses.

The image of plains Indians hunting bison on horseback factors significantly in our understanding of the history of native peoples. However, the relationship between native hunters and bison stretches much further into the story of American Indians and is very poorly appreciated. Plains Indians pursued bison on horseback for some two centuries, or slightly longer, before the buffalo's near extinction. Their ancestors hunted bison on foot for nearly 10,000 years prior to their acquisition of horses.

How could humans, propelled by legs capable of sprinting at speeds of around 20 miles per hour, successfully kill 1,000-pound animals able to run 30 miles per hour? Not only were these people able to bring down bison, they were remarkably skilled and efficient in doing so. Like their mounted successors, many of these tribes depended upon bison for the necessities of life. Their methods of killing such large, swift ungulates amply illustrate the extent to which human intelligence is able to dominate the superior physical abilities of animals.

One such technique was known as the "surround." This method involved many hunters surrounding a bison herd, or just a portion of the herd if they believed the entire band was too large to manage. The hunters would run and shout on the perimeter of the surrounded bison, slowly closing in on them from all sides. When they came close enough to the encircled animals, they shot arrows and flung lances at the bison. Animals killed on the perimeter of the trapped herd further impeded the flight of those on the inside. In a very successful surround, a few dozen or even a few hundred bison might be killed without a single escape.

A variation of the surround that involved fire was also used in some places. Fires were strategically ignited on three sides of a bison herd, leaving them a single path of escape. The ring of fire pushed the bison to waiting hunters, who blocked their flight from the flames. American Indians who inhabited the upper regions of the Mississippi River most commonly used this technique.

Early hunters also brought groups of bison within the range of their killing implements by driving them into enclosures. In some places natural features such as box canyons or steep-sided washes served as primitive corrals. Enterprising hunters also fashioned stout pens from rocks or wooden poles. These corral-like enclosures were most often used in areas where bison inhabited rocky or somewhat wooded terrain on the flanks of the mountains or in mountain valleys. Sometimes called a "pound," archaeologists have discovered enclosures that were used by tribes for many years. Working together, the party first incited a herd of bison to run, then used lines of hunters to direct buffalo into the enclosure, where they were then dispatched with arrows and spears.

Large numbers of bison were also killed at places known as *pishkuns* or buffalo jumps. A buffalo jump was simply a cliff over which a herd of bison could be driven. Animals not killed in the fall were brought down by hunters who waited at the bottom of the cliff while others caused and directed the stampede above. Some tribes were extremely diligent to kill every bison that came over the jump, believing that any survivors that escaped might warn other bison to avoid the precipitous trap in the future. Buffalo jumps occurred most frequently on the eastern front of the Rocky Mountains. The sites of hundreds of buffalo jumps are found in northern Wyoming, Montana, Saskatchewan, and Alberta.

In addition to these communal efforts to kill multiple bison, in the period prior to hunting on horseback, native hunters developed methods of stalking and killing individual animals. One widely employed technique involved a hunter draping himself in the skin of a wolf and approaching a bison herd on all fours. Buffalo were accustomed to the sight of the wolves, which were a constant presence in their world. The wolves sometimes attacked vulnerable animals, but more often simply shadowed the herds or went about the business of being a wolf. A mature bull or cow had little to fear from an

Early American Indians chased bison over cliffs at sites known as *pishkuns* or buffalo jumps. (This one is located in south-central Montana.)

individual wolf and would scarcely interrupt its grazing if such an animal came close. Native hunters used this knowledge to disguise themselves as a skulking canine and approach bison. Once within range, the hunter clad in a wolf's skin would shoot his target with an arrow.

Although the final generations of American Indians who hunted bison on horseback have most vividly captured our imagination, their skilled forebearers feasted on bison for many centuries prior to the arrival of the horse. Horses gave the native peoples more mobility, developing cultures that were more nomadic than those preceding them. But Indians had hunted bison efficiently for perhaps as long as 10,000 years before taking to the back of a mustang.

The Great Eradication

As discussed in Chapter 2, much conjecture exists regarding the number of bison in North America prior to the arrival of Europeans. The widely published figure of sixty million animals most likely traces back to estimates of bison observed by Colonel Richard Dodge on a wagon trip in Kansas in 1871. Dodge estimated both the number of the herd of bison he observed and the land area it covered. Earnest Thomas Seton, a later naturalist, extrapolated these figures to his calculation of bison range in North America, arriving at the sixty million estimate. As noted previously, more recent, scientific calculations based on range capacity, competition with other grazers, and fluctuations in precipitation and winter severity have concluded that half that many (or fewer) bison actually occupied the continent.

Whatever their historic numbers, the collapse of the bison population in the late 1800s (particularly the 1870s) was truly dramatic. Millions of animals dwindled to a population in the United States of a few hundred in a matter of a few decades. What triggered the decline?

Much has been written about the extensive market slaughter of bison, particularly in the 1870s. Bison were killed by the tens of thousands, not for their meat, but for their hides. Leather was an important industrial commodity of the day. Buffalo leather was particularly thick and durable. It found its way into a host of products, including the broad belts that powered industrial machinery. Buffalo hides became an incredibly valuable commodity, important enough to create a rush to slaughter in the 1870s that might fruitfully be likened to the Alaskan gold rush. Most biologists and historians believe the massive slaughter of bison for their hides was the primary culprit in the population collapse.

For several decades prior to the 1870s, both American Indian and European hunters actively sold bison hides to traders to procure luxuries for themselves, such as flour, tobacco, and molasses. Although their harvest failed to rival that of the later hide boom, it exerted pressure on the bison population.

Exceptionally severe winter weather and epic storms can be fatal to even healthy adult bison.

Some experts believe that bovine diseases introduced by domestic cattle also claimed substantial numbers of bison. Subsistence hunting by American Indian tribes possibly played a role as well. Native hunters on horseback most often targeted cows for their arrows, potentially reducing the reproductive capacity of the herds they hunted. Nonetheless, subsistence hunting probably played a minor role in the bison decline in comparison to the number of animals killed for leather and other purposes.

Mother Nature was not always kind to the bison, either. Weather events and drought in the 1800s exerted downward pressure on bison numbers in some areas. For example, in 1841 a warm wind during the winter melted the top layer of snow in bison habitat in Wyoming. A cold snap followed, turning the softened snow to a rock-hard crust of ice. Unable to reach the grass underneath, bison died in untold numbers. In the spring of 1844, an unusually heavy snowstorm in eastern Colorado was responsible for a massive die-off of bison.

Bison and Us

Bounding back from the brink of extinction not much more than a century ago, about 430,000 bison are estimated to now live in the United States and Canada. While their survival is no longer a question, their dual status as livestock and wild animal makes them unique among North American mammals. Other wild ungulates such as elk and whitetail deer are kept on farms, yet their numbers in the wild vastly outnumber those in domestic operations. Bison are just the opposite. Over a dozen times as many bison are contained in livestock operations than are kept for conservation purposes or roam public lands as "wild" herds.

Over the past few decades, the number of bison kept as livestock has expanded rapidly. Sales of bison meat at retail outlets and in the restaurant market totaled around $278 million in 2011. Bison meat is normally marketed as a natural meat free of growth hormones. Buffalo meat has less fat, cholesterol, and calories per ounce than beef, pork, or even skinless chicken. Many

By the time the bison was chosen as a symbol for the Wyoming state flag in 1917, the species had made a significant recovery.

consumers thus regard bison as a healthier alternative to these traditional meats. However, it is substantially more expensive. Bison may sell for twice as much as beef for equivalent cuts of meat. Most agricultural economists view the buffalo livestock industry as a business in its infancy. Whether or not demand for the meat will sustain the current numbers of bison kept as livestock remains to be seen.

Public bison herds at national wildlife refuges, along with state and national parks, are presently very healthy and generally expanding. Numerous American Indian tribes now have bison herds of their own that graze on tribal lands. The Crow tribe in south-central Montana has a substantial free-ranging herd that roams the northern flanks of the Bighorn

Many wildlife advocates believe the restoration of the bison will not truly be complete until more free-ranging herds of these iconic animals have been established on public lands in the contiguous United States.

FREE-RANGING BISON IN NORTHEASTERN MONTANA?

Many people share the desire to establish additional free-ranging bison herds in the United States. Some individuals and conservation groups have identified the Charles M. Russell National Wildlife Refuge (CMR) in northeastern Montana as an ideal place to reintroduce bison to their historic range in an unfenced setting. The refuge sprawls across 1.1 million acres of land. Surely that's enough room for a herd of bison.

Perhaps not. Some ranchers in the area and an assortment of politicians oppose the reintroduction. They fear introducing bison may lead to other restrictions on adjacent public lands. They also voice concern over the large animals competing with cattle for forage and damaging fences. Additionally they point out that bison might carry diseases to area cattle.

To some extent these criticisms are rooted in fact. Bison have no difficulty plowing through the common barbwire fences that confine cattle. Their presence would also likely reduce the number of grazing allotments on public lands available to ranchers around the wildlife refuge. However, proponents argue that cattle do not have any sacred status on public lands and that the northeastern Montana grass in question should go to whichever animal best promotes the public interest. On the CMR, they feel, that animal is the bison. If disease-free bison were introduced, the likelihood of transmitting illnesses to cattle would be absent or very small.

Will bison once again roam along the Missouri River in northeastern Montana as they did in the days of Lewis and Clark? Who knows? But given what appears to be an increasing level of support for establishing additional free-ranging bison herds in the United States, the question is probably not a matter of if, but when and where.

Mountains. Most publically kept bison herds produce more offspring than their range can support. Excess animals are often sold at public auctions.

Despite the success of bison restoration over the past century, many biologists feel the comeback of these animals in the United States is still lacking. Just two truly free-ranging bison herds occupy public lands in the Lower 48, those in Yellowstone National Park and in the Henry Mountains in Utah. Although bison in such large reserves as South Dakota's Custer State Park may range over 71,000 acres, these wild animals are ultimately confined behind a towering woven-wire fence. In the minds of some, the restoration of bison in America will not be complete until additional free-ranging herds track more of their native habitat on public lands.

Index

About the Author

A writer, photographer, and naturalist, Jack Ballard is a frequent contributor to numerous regional and national publications. He covers a variety of outdoor, conservation, and wildlife topics. He has written hundreds of articles on wildlife or wildlife-related topics, appearing in such magazines as *Colorado Outdoors, Camping Life, Wyoming Wildlife,* and many others.

Jack's photos have been published in numerous books (for Smithsonian Press, Heinemann Library, and others), calendars, and magazines. He has received multiple awards for his writing and photography from the Outdoor Writers Association of America and other professional organizations. He holds two master's degrees and is an accomplished public speaker, entertaining students, conference attendees, and recreation/conservation groups with his compelling narratives. When not wandering the backcountry, he hangs his hat in Red Lodge, Montana. See more of his work at jackballard.com.